Where Is the Amazon?

by Sarah Fabiny

illustrated by Daniel Colón

Penguin Workshop
An Imprint of Penguin Random House

For Mary Kay Bissell, who encouraged
me to discover the world—SF

To my family in Puerto Rico, who showed
me the beauty of El Yunque—DC

PENGUIN WORKSHOP
Penguin Young Readers Group
An Imprint of Penguin Random House LLC

Text copyright © 2016 by Sarah Fabiny. Illustrations copyright © 2016 by
Penguin Random House LLC. All rights reserved. Published by Penguin Workshop, an
imprint of Penguin Random House LLC, 345 Hudson Street, New York, New York 10014.
PENGUIN and PENGUIN WORKSHOP are trademarks of Penguin Books Ltd.
WHO HQ & Design is a registered trademark of Penguin Random House LLC.
Printed in the USA

Library of Congress Control Number: 2016009273

ISBN 9780448488264 (paperback)   10 9 8 7 6
ISBN 9780399542336 (library binding)   10 9 8 7 6 5 4 3 2 1

Contents

Where Is the Amazon?

On August 26, 1542, Francisco de Orellana, a Spanish explorer, and his crew finally arrived at the Atlantic Ocean. They had been sailing down a mighty river in South America. The journey had lasted more than two hundred days. The river and the surrounding landscape were like nothing they had ever come across. The river was so wide that they could not see across it in places. And the creatures swinging in the trees, splashing in the water, and flying through the sky were not like the creatures in Spain.

When Orellana and his men arrived back in Spain, Orellana told stories about their incredible journey to anyone who would listen. And it was no wonder why—the river that Orellana and his men had traveled down was the Amazon. And the surrounding landscape was the Amazon rain forest.

The Amazon is truly one of the natural wonders of the planet. Although not the longest river in the world, it carries more water than the Nile, the Mississippi, and the Yangtze combined. The river has about fifteen thousand tributaries (rivers and streams) that flow into it. Four of them are each more than one thousand miles long.

This incredible river flows through a rain forest that is probably the oldest in the world. (A rain forest is a forest with tall trees; a warm, humid climate; and lots of rain.) The Amazon rain forest includes areas of nine South American countries: Brazil, Peru, Colombia, Venezuela, Ecuador, Bolivia, Guyana, Suriname, and French Guiana. And it covers an area the size of the United States, not including Alaska and Hawaii. Scientists believe there may be around 400 billion individual trees in the rain forest. That's more than a thousand trees for every person in the United States.

GUYANA
SURINAME
FRENCH GUIANA
VENEZUELA
COLOMBIA
ECUADOR
AMAZON RIVER
B R A Z I L
P E R U
BOLIVIA
PARAGUAY
CHILE
URUGUAY
ARGENTINA

Since Francisco de Orellana's time, the Amazon River and the rain forest have been explored by thousands of people. The plants, animals, and people living in this part of the world have captured the interest of scientists, explorers, and tourists. It may seem that after almost five hundred years, there would be no more to learn. But the Amazon is special. What we are discovering is that there will always be more to discover about this incredible place.

CHAPTER 1
The River Changes Course

The mighty Amazon River starts high up in the Andes Mountains in Peru along the west coast of South America. The river then flows east for more than four thousand miles across South America and empties into the Atlantic Ocean off the coast of Brazil.

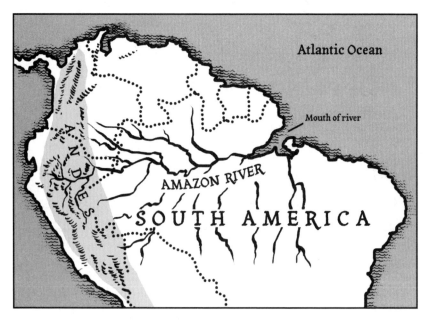

Savanna and rain forest

The Amazon didn't always flow east. It used to flow westward and emptied into the Pacific Ocean. However, the formation of the Andes Mountains, about fifteen million years ago, led to the river changing direction. The mountains blocked the flow of the Amazon. It became a sea—a huge inland body of water. Over a long period of time, this inland sea gradually changed to into a massive swampy lake.

The environment of the area also changed during this time. For millions of years, much of the land around the Amazon River had been a mix of rain forests (wet forests) and savannas (dry grasslands). But when the river got blocked up, much of the savannas became rain forest. More rain fell in the area, which meant more plants, bushes, and trees grew there. The climate became hot and humid.

The Earth's Plates

The surface of the earth is made up of eight major plates. These plates are like the skin of the planet. They are always moving, but at a very slow pace— only a couple of inches each year. The collision of two plates is what created the Andes Mountains fifteen million years ago.

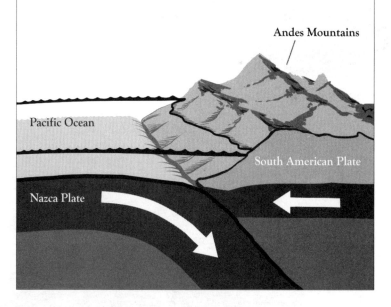

Andes Mountains

Pacific Ocean

South American Plate

Nazca Plate

About ten million years ago, the water in the freshwater lake slowly worked its way through the sandstone at the bottom. The water was able to start moving. The lake became a river again. Only this time it was flowing eastward.

CHAPTER 2
First Settlers

The first settlers probably arrived in the Amazon about twenty-five thousand to thirty thousand years ago. They came from the north of Asia and traveled across a frozen sea that linked Asia and North America. Over time, they made their way south to the tropical region surrounding the Amazon. No other humans were there, and these first settlers quickly spread out to cover a large part of what is now Central and South America.

These people were hunter-gatherers. They lived on whatever animals they could kill and whatever plants they found in the wild. They did not raise animals or grow crops.

ASIA

Bering Strait

NORTH
AMERICA

ATLANTIC
OCEAN

PACIFIC
OCEAN

SOUTH
AMERICA

Route of first settlers

13

The trees provided fuel for the fires that cooked their food and kept them warm. They also provided wood for building their homes. Once the food sources in an area were used up, the hunter-gatherers moved on to a new place.

Over time some settlers started clearing land in the rain forest for farming. They raised animals and grew crops. They didn't need to move from place to place anymore. Since that time thousands of years ago, people living in the

Amazon have adapted to this hot, humid climate. They are at home in this unique environment. There are ancient cave paintings in Brazil that were done more than ten thousand years ago. That is more than five thousand years before the Egyptians built the Great Pyramids!

CHAPTER 3
Search for the City of Gold

After Christopher Columbus's voyages across the Atlantic in the 1490s, the Spanish wanted to explore more of the "New World." Columbus and his crew had reported it was filled with riches, including spices, gemstones, and silver. The reports also included a tale about "El Dorado," a city filled with gold and jewels.

Christopher
Columbus

According to legends, the city was ruled
by a king who covered himself with gold dust
every morning. The king would then dive into
a sacred lake to wash off the dust. Afterward,
he would toss gold back into the water as an
offering to the gods.

Bands of Spanish soldiers, called conquistadors (say kon-KEE-sta-doors) were inspired by these wild stories. They set sail for the New World. They wanted to claim the land and the treasure of gold and jewels for themselves.

The first Europeans to see the Amazon were led by the Spanish commander Vicente Yáñez Pinzón (say vee-SEN-tuh YAH-nez pin-zon). In 1492, he had sailed with Christopher Columbus to the West Indies. He was the captain of the *Niña*. Seven years later, in 1499, he got the Spanish court to pay for him to do more exploring.

Pinzón began a voyage of his own to the New World. He landed on the shores of Brazil on January 26, 1500. He sailed west along the coast. In time he and his crew entered the mouth of the Amazon River. The map Pinzón had was all wrong. He thought he was in Asia, not South America.

Vicente Yáñez Pinzón

So Pinzón first thought the river was the Ganges in India. He named the river Rio Santa Maria de la Mar Dulce (River of Saint Mary of the Sweet Sea).

Pinzón and his men sailed up the Amazon for only a short distance. Then they turned around and headed back to the Atlantic. They decided to keep sailing up the coast of South America. There they came upon a native tribe called the Arawaks. Now they got just what they were looking for. Treasure!

By trading items they had brought with them, Pinzón and his crew acquired not just gold but emeralds and pearls. Pinzón was sure to be seen as a hero when he returned home.

He might not have found El Dorado, but his ship was full of riches. However, bad luck struck as Pinzón and his crew headed back to Spain. The ship was caught in a hurricane and sank—along with all the treasure! Pinzón did make it home, but with only stories to tell of his adventures.

Francisco de Orellana

Quito, Ecuador

It wasn't until 1541 that explorers learned the full length of the Amazon. In that year, Francisco de Orellana set sail from Quito, Ecuador. The city sits high up in the Andes Mountains on the west coast of South America. Orellana was with a group of conquistadors. Like Pinzón, they hoped to discover El Dorado. They were also looking for La Canela, a land filled with trees that produced a valuable spice—cinnamon!

Several years earlier, Orellana had helped Francisco Pizarro conquer the Inca Empire. On this new mission, he was working for Pizarro's brother Gonzalo.

The Age of Exploration

This is a period in history that began in the early 1400s and lasted through the 1600s. It began when Europeans set off in search of new and faster routes to the Far East—India and China. There they hoped to find riches and treasures. Some explorers set sail so that they could discover more of the world and map new areas. The Portuguese started this period of exploration under Prince Henry the Navigator. But soon the Spanish, Dutch, and English were also sending ships to make claims on the New World.

Prince Henry
the Navigator

The explorers spent weeks making their way through the dense jungle. Many of the men died from the cold in the mountains or the heat in the rain forest. They were also running out of supplies. Orellana and a group of fifty men were sent to look for food. The men headed down the Napo River, which is in modern-day Ecuador, on a small barge. When Orellana didn't return, Gonzalo Pizarro thought that they had been killed.

But Orellana and his men were alive. And the Napo River took them down into the Amazon. So although they did not find La Canela or El Dorado, they were the first Europeans to come upon the mighty river. The Amazon had a much stronger current than the Napo, and Orellana's group were unable to turn back. Luckily the men came upon a friendly group of natives in a small village. The natives offered them shelter and food.

Orellana and his men built themselves a larger boat. It was able to withstand the faster, more dangerous waters of the Amazon. For almost eight months they sailed down the river. Not only did the men have to battle treacherous waters, along the way they were attacked many times by hostile tribes. Orellana and his men claimed that one of these tribes was led by a group of fierce female warriors. It's incredible that the men actually lived to tell their tale!

The conquistadors finally arrived at the Atlantic Ocean on August 26, 1542. Orellana named the river Rio de Orellana after himself. He felt he deserved the honor! Orellana then sailed along the coast to what is now Venezuela, and then back to Spain.

On his return, Orellana told the tales of his adventures to the king of Spain. The tales included the story of how Orellana's men had been attacked by women who used clubs and bows and arrows. The king knew the ancient Greek myth of Amazon warrior women. So he proclaimed that from then on, the river should be called *Amazonas*.

The king made Orellana the governor of the region. He ordered Orellana to return and conquer it for Spain. Orellana did go back. But in 1546 he fell sick and died as he explored the mouth of the Amazon River.

Almost one hundred years later, Pedro

Pedro Teixeira

Teixeira (say TAY-shay-rah) led the next great trip along the Amazon River. Teixeira was from Portugal. He and his men were sent by their king. They were also supposed to stop Spain from claiming any more land.

Teixeira and his men sailed upriver from Belém, near the mouth of the river. The Spanish soldiers let Teixeira and his men travel along the river, but they did not like it. The Spanish considered the Amazon theirs. They didn't want the Portuguese making claims to land that belonged to them!

Teixeira and his crew arrived in Quito, but they got no further. The Spanish authorities held them there for several weeks. In the end the Spanish decided to send Teixeira and his crew back the way they came. A group of Spanish priests was sent with them.

The priests were not there to listen to the explorers' prayers. They were spies! The priests were to report back on how much of the Amazon had been settled by the Portuguese.

Spain and Portugal were determined to claim as much land as possible for themselves in this part of the New World. In 1750, the Spanish

finally agreed to Portugal's claim to most of the
Amazon River basin.

The Amazons

According to the ancient Greeks, the Amazons were a race of women warriors who were fierce, proud, and powerful. They were said to be descended from Ares, the god of war, and it was their custom to bring up only female children. Any sons born to the Amazons were either sent away to the neighboring nations or put to death. From childhood, the girls were taught to fight. The bow and arrow, the *labrys* (a kind of double-headed ax), and a shield in the shape of a crescent were their weapons. The Amazons also showed great skill as horse tamers and riders. Although there is no proof that this race of female warriors actually existed, the legend of the Amazons lived on long after the time of the ancient Greeks.

CHAPTER 4
More Discoveries

There were many more European explorers after Orellana and Teixeira who hoped to find El Dorado. They made their way to South America and searched along the Amazon River and in the surrounding rain forest. But the mythical city remained just a tale. Even so, people kept coming to the region for other reasons.

Spain and Portugal were Catholic countries. Their rulers hoped to bring Christianity to the native people in the New World. So the next accounts of the Amazon came from missionaries. (Missionaries are people sent to bring their religion to other parts of the world.)

Many Catholic missionaries traveled on the Amazon's tributaries and deep into the rain forest.

ATLANTIC OCEAN

GUYANA

SURINAME

FRENCH GUIANA

AMAZON RIVER

BELEM

MANAUS

SANTARÉM

AMAZON RIVER

BRAZIL

Map illustration by Abi Daker. © Penguin Random House LLC.

Photo © Thinkstock, photographed by quickshooting

Colorful macaws in the Amazon canopy

The Amazon rain forest's
understory and forest floor

A town along the Amazon R

© Thinkstock, photographed by Matt Gibson

iver

A jaguar on the forest floor of the Amazon

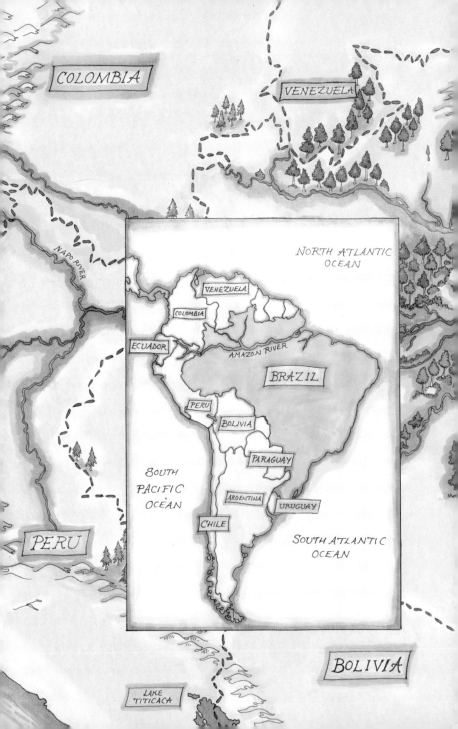

They did not always succeed in converting the native people, but they did map a large area of the Amazon. They also made detailed records of the plants and animals they found. These maps and records were useful to scientists who sailed to the Amazon years later.

The first "modern" scientific exploration of the Amazon region began in 1799. Alexander von Humboldt was in charge. He was a German explorer and a naturalist. A naturalist is someone who studies plants and animals and how they live in nature. Humboldt is considered

Alexander von Humboldt

to be the founder of modern geography.

From 1799 to 1804 Humboldt traveled about six thousand miles through Central and South America. His friend Aimé Bonpland, who was a French doctor and botanist, traveled with him. Humboldt was amazed at how animals and not man ruled the area. He wrote in his journal "Alligators and boas are masters of the river; the jaguar, the peccary, the tapir, and the monkeys traverse the forest without fear and without danger. . . . We seek in vain traces of the power of man."

Humboldt and Bonpland explored the Amazon rain forest and many of its tributaries on foot, on horseback, and by canoe. They often relied on native tribes to guide them through the thick rain forest and along the swift rivers.

They also stayed at settlements that the
missionaries had built. The tribespeople showed
the explorers where to hang sleeping hammocks so
they could avoid getting wet during a rainstorm.
They also showed them which plants to eat to help
ward off sickness. But there was one thing that the
native people couldn't help Humboldt with.

Bugs!

One of his notes talks about the beauty of
nature but says, "To have enjoyed it fully, we
should have breathed an air clear of insects."

Toucan

The two scientists discovered thousands of plants, animals, and minerals. They were especially fascinated by the birds they saw, including the brightly colored toucans and parrots. The two men also came upon an animal that produced electricity, the electric eel.

After their journey on the rivers of the Amazon area, Humboldt and Bonpland made a trip to the Andes Mountains.

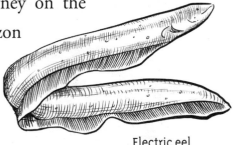
Electric eel

There they climbed Mount Chimborazo (in modern Ecuador), which is 20,702 feet high. The explorers did not make it to the summit, but they climbed to a height of 19,286 feet. That remained a world mountain-climbing record for nearly thirty years. And Humboldt and Bonpland made their climb without the help of modern mountaineering equipment, such as ropes, crampons, or oxygen tanks.

Humboldt and Bonpland's amazing journey astounded people, including Thomas Jefferson, who was president of the United States. In 1804, the explorers were invited to be guests of the president.

Thomas Jefferson

They arrived in Washington, DC, just after Jefferson had sent Lewis and Clark to explore the western United States. Humboldt and Jefferson, who was also a scientist, became good friends.

Humboldt and Bonpland's journey changed how people viewed the world. They showed how much more wildlife there was to discover on the planet. The description of their journey was written up and published in a set of books.

What they saw and recorded captured the interest of other scientists and adventurers. Many more expeditions took place after Humboldt and Bonpland published their notes.

Johann Baptist von Spix and Carl Friedrich Philip von Martius were also German naturalists. They led a group to the Amazon from 1817 to 1820. They were often ill during their journey and almost died of thirst. But they went up the Amazon River and through its rain forests as far as modern-day Peru.

Like Humboldt and Bonpland, Spix and Martius made many discoveries about plants and animals. They wanted to bring back as many specimens as possible.

They loaded a boat with an amazing collection of 6,500 species of plants, 85 species of mammals, 350 species of birds, 116 species of

Mata mata

fish, and nearly 2,700 species of insects. One of the specimens that Spix brought back to Europe was a strange-looking freshwater turtle called the mata mata. It has a flat, triangle-shaped head with a "horn" on its long snout. And one of the bird species Spix collected now bears his name—the Spix macaw. It

Spix macaw

is a small parrot with bright blue feathers.

Henry Walter Bates and Alfred Russel Wallace

In 1848, two English scientists, Henry Walter Bates and Alfred Russel Wallace, traveled to the Amazon. Bates was only twenty-three at the time, and Wallace was twenty-five. The two had met on bug-hunting walks in the English countryside. And they wanted to find new species of insects in the Amazon. Alfred Russel Wallace studied and explored the area for four years. On the journey back to England, the ship that he was on caught fire.

Wallace escaped, but all his bug collections were destroyed.

Henry Walter Bates stayed in the Amazon for eleven years. He loved birds and had a pet toucan. Bates also loved butterflies, and he had 550 new species of them in his collection. Another one of his achievements was confirming that really big spiders will kill and eat little birds.

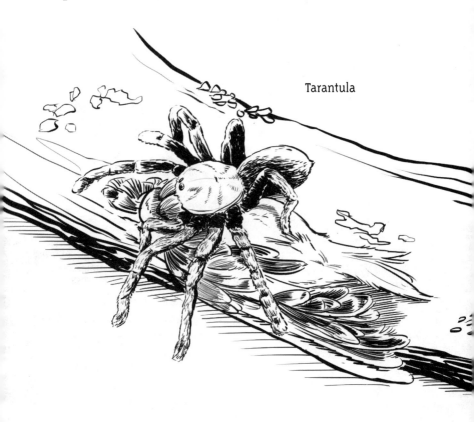

Tarantula

When he returned to England in 1859, he brought back more than 14,712 specimens. Most of these were insects. Bates had heard what had happened to Wallace on the journey back to England. So Bates sent his specimens on three separate ships.

When he got back to England, Bates spent the next three years writing about the trip. The report was called *The Naturalist on the River Amazons*. It is thought to be one of the best reports ever written on natural history travel. Charles Darwin called it "the best book of natural history travels ever published in England." Darwin and other scientists realized that the information gathered from these specimens helped explain how life on the planet developed and changed.

The Theory of Evolution

Charles Darwin is given credit for coming up with the theory of evolution. The theory describes how species have changed, developed, and adapted over time. But Alfred Russel Wallace actually came up with the theory at the same time as his colleague and friend. One day in 1858, while he was sick in bed, Wallace had an idea. He thought that species changed because the fittest individuals had characteristics that made them best able to survive and reproduce. They then passed on these characteristics to their offspring. Wallace wrote to Darwin, because he knew Darwin was interested in this subject.

Darwin had been working on the same theory for almost twenty years. Friends of both men recommended that their ideas be presented to a group of important scientists in London.

Darwin's paper was read first, and his masterpiece, *The Origin of Species*, was published the following year. From then on, Darwin overshadowed Wallace. And it has been Darwin's name that is linked with the theory of evolution. But Wallace wasn't angry or upset by this. In fact, he was Darwin's greatest supporter.

Charles Darwin

CHAPTER 5
The People of the Amazon

When European explorers arrived in the Amazon in the 1500s, none of the native tribes had ever seen armies of men dressed in armor, carrying guns, and riding horses. The tribes were often forced to help the explorers make their way up the Amazon River and through the rain forest

as they searched for riches. The native tribes knew that the fabled El Dorado—the city of gold—did not exist, but the explorers were set on finding it.

On these treasure hunts, many of the native tribespeople ended up dying. Some died from extreme cold or heat. Some died from the harsh treatment they received. The conquistadors beat them if they did not work hard enough. And they often had to go without food or water.

However, most deadly of all were the germs that the soldiers brought with them from Europe. Germs that caused smallpox, measles, and flu. The natives had never been exposed to these new diseases before, and many died from them. They knew how to use the bark, leaves, and roots of trees and plants to make medicine to help against diseases they suffered, such as malaria. But they were powerless against these new germs.

Harsh treatment of natives continued into the late 1800s. By now explorers were no longer looking for El Dorado. The new treasure they were after was rubber from rubber trees in the Amazon.

Rubber tree

Why was rubber so important? In the late nineteenth century, rubber was used for everything from waterproofing material to coating telegraph wires to manufacturing tires. To help get as much rubber as possible, the explorers enslaved many people from the native tribes. As in the Age of Exploration, many died from sickness and harsh treatment.

Hundreds of years ago, there were millions of native people in the Amazon. Today it is thought that there are just a few hundred thousand in the area. Some of the tribes have chosen to live in towns and cities in the rain forest. They live like most modern people do, with electricity and plumbing. But about fifty of the four hundred tribes do not have any contact with the outside world. And tribes are still being found in the deepest parts of the rain forest. So there is no way to tell the exact number of people who inhabit the Amazon.

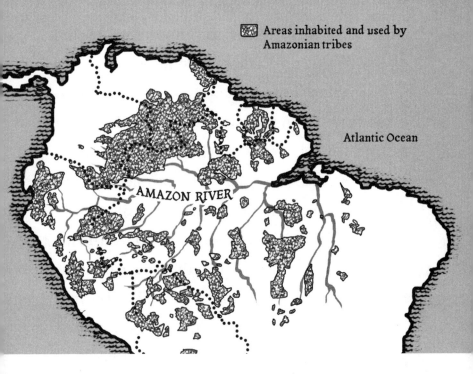

Areas inhabited and used by
Amazonian tribes

Atlantic Ocean

AMAZON RIVER

The tribes in the Amazon are very different from each other in their languages, their beliefs, and their customs. The largest tribe is the Yanomani, whose name means "fierce people." They live in northern Brazil and southern Venezuela. The tribe has around thirty thousand members, and they have contact with the outside world. Like their ancestors, they are hunter-gatherers. They often trade things they collect in the rain forest for items such as sugar, oil, and soap from stores in cities.

Tribes such as the Passé and the Yuri, who live in Colombia, have no or very little contact with the outside world. It's hard to know exactly how many members are in each tribe, but it's probably not more than a few hundred. It is believed that these tribes made their way into remote areas of the rain forest to escape the rubber boom. They did not want to work as slaves, and they did not want to catch diseases from the Europeans.

Yuri tribe

Some of the tribes in the Amazon are nomads, living in much the same way as their ancestors did thousands of years ago. They move from place to place, hunting animals, fishing, and gathering food as they travel. Animals that the tribes hunt include peccary (a type of wild pig), capybara (the largest rodent in the world), deer, and monkey.

Other tribes farm the land. They stay in the same area from season to season and year to year. The tribes live off what they grow—bananas, squash, papayas, corn, manioc (a root vegetable that is like a potato), and beans. They also grow cotton, which they use to make clothing.

Many of the Amazon tribes live in communal houses, meaning many people share one large home. These homes are often made from bamboo covered in banana or palm leaves and straw. Many of the people sleep in hammocks.

Children in most Amazon tribes do not go to formal school. Instead, when they are old enough, they are taught what they need to know from the elders of their tribe. They learn things like how to hunt, fish, and find the plants that are good to eat and provide medicine.

Boys in some tribes go through ceremonies when they reach a certain age. This is to make them strong and prove that they are now men. In the Sateré Mawé tribe, boys must wear gloves filled with bullet ants, which have a strong and painful bite.

Because it is so hot and humid in the Amazon rain forest, many of the tribes wear very little clothing, or no clothing at all! What they do wear is made from what is found in the rain forest, usually either plants or animal skins. And many of the tribes have tattoos or small sticks inserted through their noses or cheeks. This may be done to ward off evil spirits, show victory in battle, or honor the gods or heroes of the tribe.

Over the past centuries, the population of the tribes in the Amazon has decreased. Some tribes have disappeared altogether. Today the governments of the countries in the Amazon region have created programs help keep track of the number of people belonging to different tribes. They realize that the tribes are important to the Amazon and to the world.

Spirits Are Everywhere

Many tribes in the Amazon believe in animism. This is the belief that animal spirits live in all things. Everything, including vines, trees, rocks, mountains, rivers, and even wind and thunder has a soul or a spirit. Members of these tribes believe that the shaman, or spiritual leader, of the tribe is able to control and use the power of spirits. With this power he can help heal members of the tribe, cause harm to enemies, and even turn into an animal.

CHAPTER 6
Layers of a Rain Forest

Over thousands of years the tribes of the Amazon have learned to live in this unique place. The rain forest is a dense, lush environment. The climate is hot and humid. The average temperature is about 79°F. The temperature between seasons doesn't vary that much, but there is a big difference in temperature between night and day.

The area also gets a lot of rainfall—over eighty inches a year! In many areas it rains every day, and there is also a rainy season when it rains almost constantly. (In the United States, Seattle, Washington, is known as a rainy city. But it is dry compared to the Amazon! Seattle has rain about 150 days a year and gets about thirty-seven inches of rain every year.)

Because of the tropical climate and the huge amount of rainfall, the Amazon is a perfect place for plants to grow. Trees tower overhead, vines twist and hang from the branches, and very little sunlight reaches the floor of the rain forest.

Every rain forest, including the Amazon, is split into four different layers. Each layer has special conditions and is home to certain kinds of plants.

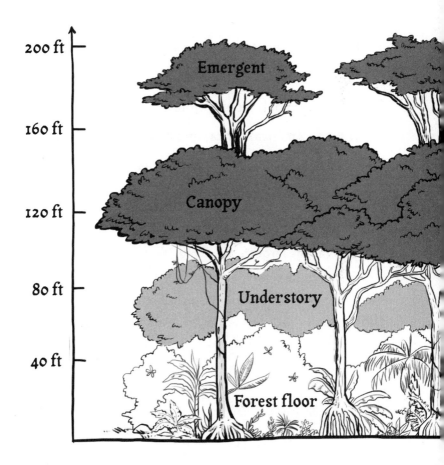

Rain Forests of the World

There are two different kinds of rain forest: tropical and temperate. Both types get lots of rain and have lots of plant and animals species, and the trees are dense, tall, and very green. Tropical rain forests are warm and humid, while temperate rain forests are cool. Tropical forests cover large parts of South America, Africa, and Asia. Temperate rain forests are found in only a few places around the world, such as the Pacific Northwest in the United States. Of all the rain forests in the world, the Amazon is by far the largest.

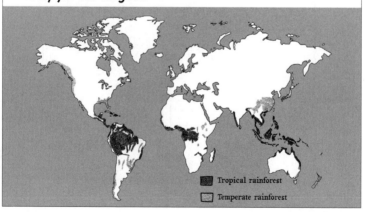

Tropical rainforest
Temperate rainforest

The emergent layer is the tallest layer in the rain forest. The trees in this layer can be two hundred feet tall (that's as tall as a twenty-story building!) and have trunks more than sixteen feet across. Sunlight and rain are plentiful in this top layer. But these trees have to endure strong winds. Butterflies, insects, birds, bats, and some small monkeys live in this layer. Most animals don't venture up this high, because the branches are unsteady and it's a long way down to the forest floor.

The next layer down is the canopy. The trees in this layer are around 100 to 150 feet tall. They form a natural roof over the two layers below. The plants and animals that live in the canopy are specially adapted for life in the trees. Dense leaves

and branches make it hard to see in this layer of the rain forest, so some animals and birds rely on loud calls or songs to communicate with each other. And many canopy creatures such as toucans, bats, and spider monkeys fly, glide, or jump from tree to tree.

Very little was known about the canopy layer of the Amazon rain forest until the 1980s. Up until then it had been too difficult and expensive to study it. Today, scientists explore the canopy using construction cranes, balloon rafts, ski-lift trams, and complex pulleys. This equipment allows them to easily make their way into this layer of the rain forest. The scientists are careful to make sure that the equipment does not cause damage to the trees or injure animals.

Many epiphytic (say ep-uh-FIT-ik) plants, or "air plants," live in the canopy layer. These plants do not need to have their roots in soil. Instead they absorb moisture and nutrients from the air. They depend on a host plant to provide support and a place to grow.

As for animals, thousands of insect species live in the rain forest canopy. This layer is also home to animals such as the bright-billed toucan, the loud howler monkey, and the slow-moving sloth.

Some sloths stay in the same tree for years. And they move so slowly that tiny algae grows on their fur. The algae makes them look greenish-gray and helps camouflage them from predators.

Sloth

Beneath the canopy is the understory. It is dark and filled with vines, shrubs, and smaller trees. The trees in this layer rarely grow more than fifteen feet tall. In some places this layer is so dense, it is impossible for people to get through. Only about 5 percent of the sunlight that reaches the canopy makes it down to the understory. Therefore, the leaves in this layer are very large so that they can collect as much sunshine as possible. Well-camouflaged jaguars spend time in this layer, since they can't climb much higher. It's also home to tree frogs, owls, snakes, and lots of insects.

The forest floor is the bottom layer. Giant anteaters and many types of snakes and termites live here. Almost no sunlight reaches the forest floor. This makes the quality of the soil poor, and almost no plants grow in this layer. However, many types of fungi live on the forest floor. The fungi help dead plants and animals decay. So does the climate.

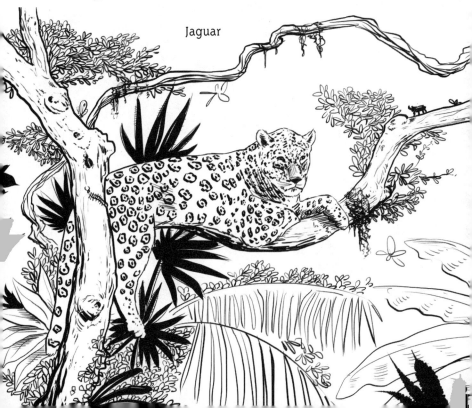

Jaguar

A dead leaf that might take a year to decompose in a regular climate will disappear in six weeks on the forest floor. The rapid decay of old plants helps new, younger plants to grow quickly, keeping the rain forest lush and green.

Giant anteater

The Cacao Tree

One type of tree native to the Amazon rain forest is the cacao tree. Its scientific name is *Theobroma cacao*, which in Latin means "food of the gods." And that's a good name for it, since cocoa beans, which are turned into chocolate, come from this tree! The cocoa beans grow inside large pods on the trees. A typical pod contains a few dozen beans. It takes several hundred beans to make one pound of chocolate. But the cacao tree doesn't just give us cocoa beans for chocolate. More than 150 chemicals are found in the leaves, pods, and bark. Native tribes use these parts of the tree to treat fever, tiredness, and coughs. Drug companies use the chemicals to make medicine for illnesses such as diabetes and heart disease.

CHAPTER 7
Incredible Creatures

The Amazon rain forest is home to all sorts of amazing animals. They range from harpy eagles that rule the sky to leafcutter ants that clean up the forest floor. Scientists are still finding new species of animals every year. In 2013, scientists discovered the olinguito (say oh-lin-GHEE-toe). A member of the raccoon family, it looks like a cross between a teddy bear and a house cat. Although it looks cute and cuddly, it has very large, sharp claws for climbing trees.

Olinguito

Why are there so many different kinds of animals living in this rain forest? It has to do with the climate. Some climates—like that of the Sahara or the Arctic—make it hard for wildlife to survive. But in the Amazon the temperatures are warm, there is plenty of rain, and there are many sources of food. There are also different ecosystems within the rain forest in which creatures can live. An ecosystem is the relationship between all the living things (plants, animals, and other organisms) and nonliving things (sun, soil, temperature) in an area. In an ecosystem, each of these living and nonliving things has a role to play.

The rain forest has just the right combination to create a perfect environment for all kinds of mammals, birds, reptiles, amphibians, fish, and insects.

There are more than 420 mammal species in the Amazon. (That's about the same number of mammal species in the United States.) The jaguar is the third-largest wild cat in the world (after lions and tigers). This big cat can weigh more than two hundred pounds, but it can still climb trees easily. It often ambushes its prey from the cover of leafy trees. Jaguars hunt deer, monkeys, tapirs, and fish. Unlike most other wild cats, jaguars do not avoid water and are good swimmers.

Birds live in every layer of the Amazon rain forest. One of the most unusual is the keel-billed toucan. It is a member of the woodpecker family. Its brightly colored bill makes it stand out in the bird world. It is usually all green, but it can be a mixture of green, yellow, blue, and orange. Even though the toucan's bill can be

Keel-billed toucan

almost eight inches long, it is very light. It is made out of keratin, the same substance that makes up human hair and fingernails.

From the huge green anaconda to the small poison dart frog, there are more than one thousand species of reptiles and amphibians in the Amazon. The green anaconda is the heaviest snake in the world, and only one snake (the reticulated python) is longer. Green anacondas can grow up to thirty feet long and weigh up to 550 pounds. (That's about the weight of three men!) These snakes spend most of their time hunting in the water. They use sight and smell to hunt, but they can also sense heat given off by their prey.

Anaconda

Once an anaconda has captured its prey, it squeezes the prey to death. The anaconda then opens its jaws so that its mouth becomes extrawide, and it swallows the prey whole—no matter the size. An anaconda can capture and eat a jaguar. And once it's had a meal that large, it can go weeks or months without eating again.

The Amazon River and the smaller rivers and streams that flow into it contain around three thousand species of freshwater fish. They range in size from the huge arapaima, which can reach a length of almost fifteen feet, to the tiny toothpick fish, which is usually only a few inches long.

One of the strangest fish that lives in the Amazon is the payara, or "vampire fish." It gets its name from the two large fangs on its lower jaw. These fangs can be four to six inches long. They are so long that there are holes in its upper jaw for them to fit into. Payaras have few enemies. They even prey on piranhas, which are known for their very sharp teeth and powerful jaws.

Payara

The number of mammals, birds, reptiles, amphibians, and fish in the Amazon is huge. But it is tiny compared to the number of insect species that live there—probably around 2.5 million! All of Europe has 321 species of butterflies. But just one national park in the Amazon rain forest has about 1,300 butterfly species. And scientists are still discovering new species of insects almost every year.

The damp and dark conditions in much of the rain forest make it the perfect place for insects. Butterflies and moths enjoy the rain, beetles and cockroaches have plenty of places to hide in the bushes and trees, and ants and grasshoppers can find plenty of food on the forest floor.

Amazing Ants

There are more than one thousand species of ants in the Amazon jungle. They range in size from just a tiny fraction of an inch long to the length of your little finger. In some ways, the ants in the Amazon keep the place running. They help keep the forest floor clean of dead and decaying material. They help pollinate plants and flowers. They protect some plants from other, destructive insects. And they are also food for many other species of insects, as well as lots of animals. Most ants live in large groups and work together to build nests and find food. In the Amazon, one kind of ant builds something called a devil's garden. These ants create a poison. The poison kills off all but one type of plant in an area. The ants use this plant for shelter and food. A devil's garden may contain three million workers and may exist for more than eight hundred years!

CHAPTER 8
Protecting the Forest

Because of its size and the many kinds of plants and animals that live there, the Amazon rain forest is like no other place on Earth. It also plays a very important role in the life of our planet. Every day, this vast forest changes a huge amount of carbon dioxide to oxygen. And nearly every creature on Earth needs oxygen to live and breathe. So the Amazon rain forest is often called the "lungs of the planet."

However, the rain forest is being cut down for lumber and to make way for industry, towns, farms, and roads. More than one-fifth of the Amazon rain forest has been destroyed. Between May 2000 and August 2005, Brazil lost more than fifty-one thousand square miles of forest—

that's an area larger than the country of Greece. And in the time it takes to read this chapter, an area of Brazil's rain forest larger than two hundred football fields will have been destroyed.

Many people feel that the Amazon rain forest is so massive that it doesn't matter if some of it is cut down. But when areas of the forest are cut down or burned, it causes species of plants and animals to become extinct. That means that they are gone forever. It also destroys the homes of the native people. As the size of the rain forest shrinks, they have fewer places to live.

And when trees are cut down, there are fewer left to absorb carbon dioxide from the atmosphere. Fewer trees result in more carbon dioxide in the air. Carbon dioxide is called a greenhouse gas, because it traps the sun's heat in the atmosphere. This causes the air temperature all around the world to go up. And this causes climate change. Climate change can bring about weather disasters, like tornadoes and hurricanes. It causes icebergs to melt at the North and South Poles. It creates drought in some places and floods in others.

The world may also miss out on discoveries of

new medicines if the Amazon rain forest continues to disappear. Less than 10 percent of the plants in the jungle have been examined. If scientists can't study the plants, they won't able to create new medicines. These medicines might help treat diseases such as cancer, diabetes, arthritis, AIDS, and Alzheimer's.

Governments all around the world have realized that it is important to protect this special river, the surrounding rain forest, and the people, animals, and plants that live there. The countries in the Amazon region have put special programs in place to preserve the area. Brazil has created the world's largest network of protected areas. Organizations in Bolivia help native tribes preserve their land and way of life. Colombia now builds roads that do the least amount of damage to the environment. There are also many organizations and charities that raise money to help preserve this special place on the planet.

How Can You Help?

Rain forests around the world, including the Amazon, are disappearing quickly. The good news is that there are many people and organizations that want to help save them. But it will not be easy, and it will take a lot of work. It may seem like small things won't make a difference. But if enough people do small things, they add up. Here are some things that you, your family and friends, and your community can do to help ensure rain forests are around for thousands of years:

Only buy chocolate, bananas, and coffee that are labeled as "fair trade." These products come from companies that don't hurt the environment.

Recycle as much as possible and use recycled paper. This will mean that fewer trees in the rain forest will be cut down.

FAIRTRADE

Encourage your parents to drive fuel-efficient cars and to keep the temperature in the house lower in the winter. Conserving energy will help slow down global warming.

If you can, make a donation to an organization that helps protect rain forests and the people, plants, and animals that live there.

CHAPTER 9
A Trip down the Amazon

Lots of scientists and researchers travel to the Amazon to study the plants, the animals, and the native tribes that live there. This beautiful area also attracts lots of tourists every year. Have you ever thought about what it would be like to travel down the Amazon River? What do you think you'd see and do on your journey?

If you flew to the Amazon rain forest, it would look like a thick green carpet of broccoli below you. That green carpet would stretch out for as far as you could see. And the Amazon River would look like a green-brown snake slithering through the carpet. When you got out of the plane, you would immediately feel the heat and humidity. The air would feel heavy and thick.

You could start your trip in Manaus, Brazil, like many tourists do. Manaus is a big port city with around two million people. It is about halfway up the river, right in the heart of the rain forest. Because of its location, many boats dock there to load and unload goods that are going into and coming out of the rain forest. It has a fancy opera house, beautiful parks, many museums, and lively markets. The city is often called "the Paris of the Jungle."

In Manaus you could board a riverboat and make your way down the river. At this point on the river, the water flows slowly, about three miles an hour. That's about the average speed of someone walking. After a couple of hours, you would come to the "meeting of the rivers." This is a spot in the Amazon where the darker waters of the smaller Rio Negro tributary meet the lighter waters of the Amazon. The darker and lighter water flow side by side without mixing for almost four miles. This is due to the differences in the temperatures,

speeds, and densities of the water. The two rivers eventually blend.

As you floated down the river, you might be lucky enough to spot an Amazon River dolphin. They are the largest freshwater dolphins in the world and can be pale blue, off-white, or even pink. You might see bright macaw parrots flying overhead and hear the calls of howler monkeys from the trees along the riverbank.

As you continued to glide down the Amazon, you would see modern villages and towns on the banks of the river. There would be boats of all sizes traveling up and down the river day and night.

As night started to fall, swarms of mosquitoes would surround the boat, and sounds of nocturnal animals (animals that are active at night) would be heard. Look carefully and you might be able to spot the eyes of a caiman—which is similar to an alligator—peeking out of the river. When it's time for bed, be sure to wrap your mosquito net around you!

There might be a chance to do some fishing as you make your way to the mouth of the Amazon. You never know what you might catch. Perhaps a bright-colored peacock bass, a strange-looking arawana, or even a piranha—watch out for the teeth!

As you head down the Amazon, you would see some incredible things. But the one thing you would never see is a bridge. Even though the river is more than four thousand miles long, there isn't a single bridge linking one side to the other!

After five or six days you would reach the mouth of the Amazon River at the Atlantic Ocean. The

mouth of the river is more than 250 miles wide. That's more than the distance between New York City and Boston! And every day the Amazon empties 4.5 trillion gallons of water into the Atlantic Ocean. That's enough water to supply every home in the United States for more than five months.

What a fantastic journey on an incredible river
in an amazing rain forest!

Ecotourism

Many people want to visit all the amazing spots on this planet. It is getting easier to travel to every part of the world to see these wonders. But the more people travel to places, the more chance there is of those places being harmed or destroyed. Many special places become polluted because of the number of tourists who visit. Or places that were hard to get to now have busy roads and airports.

Or forests are cut down to make room for hotels and more tourists.

If you are lucky enough to visit a special place in the world, you could be an ecotourist. That means you are mindful about the natural environment and all the plants, animals, and people living there. You stay in hotels, take tours, and buy souvenirs that help the local community and don't harm the environment. It's a great way to see the wonders of the world and help preserve them at the same time.

Timeline of the Amazon

c. 30,000 BC	Settlers arrive in the Amazon River basin
AD 1492	Christopher Columbus sails to the New World
1500	Vicente Yáñez Pinzón sails into the Amazon
1532	The Inca Empire falls to Francisco Pizarro
1541	Francisco de Orellana sails down the lower half of the Amazon River
1542	Orellana and his men reach the mouth of the Amazon River
1637	Pedro Teixeira explores the full length of the Amazon River
1799–1804	First modern scientific exploration of the Amazon
1817–1820	Johann Baptist von Spix and Carl Friedrich Philip von Martius lead an expedition to the Amazon region and collect thousands of specimens
1848	Henry Walter Bates and Alfred Russel Wallace explore the Amazon
1850s–1920s	Rubber boom in the Amazon River basin
1863	Henry Walter Bates publishes *The Naturalist on the River Amazons*
1970	Trans-Amazonian Highway project begins
2009	The World Social Forum in Brazil focuses on the ecological crises facing the Amazon
2010	Worst drought in fifty-five years hits the Amazon Basin
2013	Researchers estimate there are 400 billion trees in the Amazon rain forest, divided into 16,000 different species

Timeline of the World

c. 3150 BC	Start of ancient Egyptian civilization
776 BC	First Olympic Games
c. 27 BC	Start of the ancient Roman Empire
AD 1095	Start of the Crusades
1620	Pilgrims sail from England to North America on the *Mayflower*
1789	Start of the French Revolution
1803	Louisiana Purchase doubles the size of the United States
1861	Start of the US Civil War
1863	US President Abraham Lincoln issues the Emancipation Proclamation
1876	Alexander Graham Bell is granted a patent for the telephone
1911	Roald Amundsen reaches the South Pole
1945	End of World War II
1953	Edmund Hillary and Tenzing Norgay reach the summit of Mount Everest
1969	Neil Armstrong becomes the first person to walk on the moon
1994	Nelson Mandela elected president of South Africa
2008	Barack Obama elected president of the United States

Bibliography

*Books for young readers

*Cooke, Tim. *The Exploration of South America.* New York: Gareth Stevens Publishing, 2013.

*Gates, Phil. *Terror on the Amazon: The Quest for El Dorado.* New York: DK Publishing, 2000.

Hemming, John. *Tree of Rivers: The Story of the Amazon.* New York: Thames and Hudson, 2009.

*Osborne, Will, and Mary Pope Osborne. *Magic Tree House Research Guide: Rain Forests.* New York: Scholastic, 2001.

*Rice, William B. *Time for Kids: Amazon Rainforest.* Huntington Beach, CA: Teacher Created Materials, 2012.

Van Dyk, Jere. "The Amazon: South America's River Road." *National Geographic*, February 1995, 2–39.

WEBSITES

amazon-rainforest.org/indigenous-tribes.html

nationalzoo.si.edu/animals/amazonia/facts/basinfacts.cfm

newworldencyclopedia.org/entry/Amazon_River

projectamazonas.org/brief-history-amazon-exploration

rainforests.mongabay.com/amazon

worldwildlife.org/places/amazon